A Diamond in the Rough

A love story

By Anna Johnson

A DIAMOND IN THE ROUGH: A LOVE STORY
By Anna Johnson
Copyright © 2026
Published by
En'spired Publishing, LLC

EP@enspiredpublishing.com
www.enspiredpublishing.com
Editing by Nora Anderson(@andersonben190)
Book cover & Illustration by Diocellina Padillia Jr
Diocejrpadilla@gmail.com

Print ISBN#979-8-9925805-7-0
eBook ISBN#979-8-9925805-9-4

Introduction

A Diamond in the Rough: A Love Story

is a love story about two imperfect people who found each other at exactly the right time, even though neither of them was shining brightly when they met. Both carried their own struggles. Neither looked perfect nor felt flawless. But instead of giving up, they chose to stay, to fight for each other, and to face every challenge side by side. Through patience, effort, and a lot of heart, they overcame obstacle after obstacle and built a strong, loving partnership, one that grew into a beautiful, blended family.

Acknowledgment

I want to begin by thanking Jesus for being the head of my life. I thank God for directing and guiding me in every step and every decision. I am also grateful to God for blessing me with the best parents a girl could ever ask for. My dad was the perfect example of a man who knew how to lovingly blend a family and raise children in a nurturing home. My mom taught me how to be a caring, devoted mother and how to ensure my children and my husband are always taken care of.

I want to thank my husband for being the love of my life, the best father to our children, and my best friend and biggest cheerleader. He supports everything I even think about doing, and I love him deeply for his constant, unconditional love. I am also grateful to my husband's parents for blessing me with such a wonderful husband and for raising such an amazing man.

I also want to thank my children and my granddaughter for their love, support, and encouragement. I love you all so much, and I am truly grateful to be your mother and grandmother.

I want to thank my marriage role models, whose relationships have inspired and encouraged me along the way. My sisters, both by blood and by love, and their husbands: Diane and Donell, Mary and David, Heather and John, Wanda and Terry, and my Auntie Shug and Uncle Johnny. Your examples of commitment and love have been a blessing to us. We appreciate each and every one of you.

Lastly, I want to thank all the people who have prayed for us, supported us, encouraged us, and loved us throughout our lives, including our cousins, nieces, nephews, aunts, uncles, relatives, and friends. We appreciate each and every one of you.

Contents

Chapter 1

Exploration: Exploring a New Direction

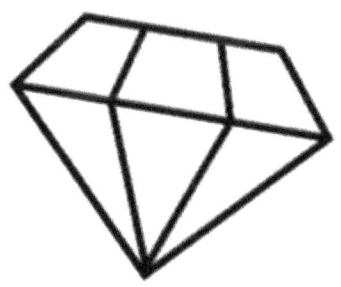

Man, how did I let this happen? I remember when I bought this house, I was so excited and felt so accomplished. Now, four years later, I am selling it. Thank God I was able to sell it and avoid foreclosure. The bank was threatening me with foreclosure, but by the grace of God, an attorney fought for me, and I was able to sell the house and get some money out of it. It is a blessing to work at a law school and receive help from the attorneys. However, I still feel so disappointed in myself because now my girls and I must move back to the city and get an apartment. I am just praying that the next time I get a home, it will be with my husband, in Jesus' name.

These were my thoughts as I stood on the corner of Lasalle and Jackson, just leaving the closing after selling my first home.

After closing, I pick up the girls from after-school care so we can head over to my sister's house. I have two girls: my oldest is Jasmine, who is thirteen, and my youngest is Ashley, who is seven. My apartment will not be ready for another week, so we had to stay with my sister and her family. This was not ideal for the girls or for me, and I could not wait until my place was ready. I prayed my landlord would have it finished by the end of the week because we were used to having our own space. We had to sleep in my sister's basement on her couches while we waited for the apartment to be ready. Staying with my sister made me feel like a failure, and I promised myself that first night that I would never be in a situation where I had to live with anyone again.

Before the end of the week, the landlord called and said we could move in early because the apartment was ready.

I could not wait until the weekend. I decided to get some blankets and a TV from the storage unit, and we were going to move in that night. We went to the apartment, and the girls and I slept on the floor until the movers came on Monday morning. We were so excited to be moving back into our own space again. I stopped to get pizza and snacks for dinner that night. This gave me time to start cleaning and getting the girls' rooms together. I did not like being back in the city, but I promised myself we would only be here for one year. Although it was a big and nice apartment, I could not stand the city.

The movers came on Monday, and now we were all moved in. Both girls had their own bedrooms, and my oldest daughter's room had an enclosed back porch attached. She called that space her sitting room. Jasmine loved writing poetry, so it was the perfect place for her to write. My bedroom was toward the front of the apartment. It was a nice size and fit all of my belongings. The downside was that the apartment was on Austin Boulevard, a main street on the west side of Chicago, and it was always busy. I could hear buses, police sirens, and crackheads all night long. Another issue was that we had to go to the laundromat to wash our clothes every week. I had never lived without my own washer or dryer, so this was going to be an adjustment. My landlord said I could use the washer and dryer in her building two doors down, but I figured that if I was going to haul laundry, I might as well take it to the laundromat and wash everything at once. That weekend, I planned to look for a nice laundromat, probably somewhere in Oak Park.

3

Laundry day came, and I found a great little laundromat in Oak Park. An older couple owned it, and it was clean with a parking lot in the back. I enjoyed doing laundry there because it was always clean, and if you went early in the morning, no one else was around. I usually brought something to read or spent time with the girls. There was an ice cream and coffee shop next door and a Giordano's pizza across the street. There was also a convenience store nearby where I would sometimes buy the girls chips. Every Saturday morning became our laundry time, and it usually took a couple of hours. After that, we had the rest of the day to ourselves.

A couple of months passed in the apartment, and once again it was Saturday morning, which meant laundry day. Most of the time, I was eager to get it done, but this morning I was not in the mood. I put my hair up in a ponytail, skipped the makeup, and decided to just get it over with. I pulled up, parked, and started taking the clothes out of the trunk. Then I heard, "Good morning." I turned and saw a guy standing behind the ice cream and coffee shop, smoking a cigarette. I said good morning and kept unloading the car. He said, "Today is the day for laundry, huh?" I said yes, smiled, and continued what I was doing. He kept talking and mentioned that he needed to do laundry too. All I could think was, will this guy leave me alone? I was not in the mood that morning. Still, he was polite and not yelling anything inappropriate, so I told myself to just be nice. He continued talking casually, and in my mind, I figured he was just being friendly.

I finished my brief conversation with the guy and headed inside to start my laundry for the week. My oldest daughter started laughing at me.

"What are you laughing at?" I asked.

"At you," she said.

"Why?"

"Because that guy is flirting with you."

I said, "Girl, no, he is not. He is just being a nice guy. If he were flirting, he would have asked for my name, phone number, or something." Both girls started laughing like I was completely clueless. I laughed at myself, wondering if I was disconnected from flirting. It had been a long time since I had been with a man. I had given up on dating and decided I would be the best mom I could be to my girls. In my mind, it was just them and me against the world. Plus, I was looking a mess that day. I am already a full-figured woman, I am also dark-skinned, and I had my braids up in a ponytail with no makeup. I was not feeling pretty at all.

We finished the laundry and started loading the car. As we approached it, I saw the guy standing outside again. He said hello to my girls, and they got into the car. In my mind, I thought, this guy is definitely flirting now. He said, "You should bring your girls over here sometime for some ice cream." I said okay, maybe one day. Then he said, "Let me give you my phone number so we can make that happen. My name is Jeremy, and here is my home and work phone number."

In my mind, I was thinking, wow, this guy is giving me his actual phone number and work number. Nobody does that anymore, so he really wants to talk to me. He did not ask for my number, which surprised me too. I said okay and took his information. My girls were laughing and said, "I told you he was flirting."

The following week, I continued with my full-time job and took the girls to and from school and their after-school activities. I was also in school working toward my bachelor's degree, so two days a week after work, I went straight to class. Easter was coming up, so for the next couple of weeks, I went to the laundromat later in the evening and did not see my new friend. One day, while cleaning out my purse, I noticed the phone number he had given me. I was relaxing at home that day, so I decided to call him and see if he really had been flirting.

As soon as he answered and I said hello, he said, "Hello, Samantha. I have been hoping you would call me." I was stunned and could not believe he remembered my name after two weeks. He also sounded genuinely excited to hear from me. We talked for a while about what we had both been doing, and the conversation flowed easily from the very beginning.

I eventually gave him my phone number, including my work number. He told me he was living in a halfway house not far from where I lived. At first, that made me nervous, but he explained that he had recently moved back to Chicago from California and found out that his mom and stepdad were moving to Michigan. He ended up with nowhere to live and was able to rent a room there. He was also enrolled at Harold Washington Community College downtown. I thought it was great that he was working and going to school because I was doing the same. He also shared right away that he had two biological sons and another son who was not biologically his but whom he raised as his own. I thought, wow, this guy seems to have a good heart, even though he looks like a roughneck. He was tall, muscular, handsome, with a chiseled face, and he wore Timberlands, just like I liked. I thought, dear God, you know what I like, thank you.

One day, he called me at work and told me he was downtown at Harold Washington College. I asked what time he would be finished, and he said around 5:00 p.m. I asked if he could wait until about 5:15 p.m. and said I would pick him up and give him a ride home since we lived close to each other. He said, "For real? You will give me a ride home?" I did not know what to think about that response, but I really wanted to see what this guy was about. I also knew I could be a little late because my sister had picked up the girls and was taking them to the movies. I told him I would be there and to stand on the corner. He said okay, and I was excited to see him again.

I could not wait to get out of work that day to see Jeremy. Before leaving, I went to the bathroom, checked my hair, and put on some makeup. I made sure my breath was fresh and my teeth were clean. I had butterflies in my stomach on the way there. Then I started to think, what if he is a serial killer and does something to me? But I remembered how open he had been about himself and his life, so I told myself he could not be that bad. As I pulled up to the corner of Lake and State Street, I saw Jeremy. Oh my God, I had forgotten how nice his body was. He looked strong and handsome, and every part of me felt excited, if you know what I mean.

He got in the car, gave me the nicest hug, and immediately said, "Thank you for picking me up." He then told me he could not believe I would give him a ride home. I told him, "Why not? It's not like I'm going out of my way." Plus, it gave us a chance to talk face to face. That is exactly what we did the entire drive to the halfway house. He told me about his life in California and his childhood growing up on the south side of Chicago. We talked about being parents and how much he loved his boys. He also shared that living in the halfway house was temporary and that he was actively looking for a place of his own.

We sat in the car for about thirty minutes, talking and sharing. He never tried to touch me or do anything inappropriate. We genuinely enjoyed learning about each other. I think I was the naughty one because I kept looking at his chest and imagining him naked and what we could do together. I often had to pull myself back and focus on the conversation. Then I thought, okay, this guy is too good to be true, so let me see how he would handle Jesus. I invited him to go to church with the girls and me for Easter. I figured that if he liked me, I should see early on how he felt about my kids. I was sure this would make him run, but it didn't. He simply said okay and asked what time he should be ready. Once again, I was shocked and could not wait to see him on Sunday.

8

Easter Sunday came, and I called him that morning to wake him up, but he didn't answer. I kept calling, but still no response, so I went to church without him. All day, I wondered what had happened and why he had ghosted me. After church, I took the girls to hang out with their cousins for the afternoon. I told my cousin I would pick them up later and that I was going home to work on some homework. Jeremy was on my mind, and I wanted to see him.

I took a chance and drove to the halfway house where I had dropped him off. He came downstairs, gave me a big hug, and immediately apologized for missing church. He told me he had overslept and didn't hear his alarm. He promised he would go with us next time, and I told him no worries. At that moment, my thoughts were elsewhere. I asked if he wanted to come over to my place for a little while. I explained that the girls were with family and that I had some time alone. He immediately said yes, and we headed to my place.

When we arrived, we sat down and started talking. He asked if he could use my phone and called his dad. While talking, he told him he was at his girlfriend's house. I looked up in shock and said, "When did I become your girlfriend?" After he hung up, I asked him the same question. He said, "Right now," and asked if that was okay with me. I didn't argue. I just started kissing him. One thing led to another, and we both enjoyed our first encounter. Afterward, I dropped him back off and went to pick up my girls.

About six weeks had passed since that encounter. We were spending time together about once a week, but we talked every day. During this time, I began noticing some things, though I wasn't completely sure what to make of them. One day, he called and asked to borrow ten dollars. I thought that was strange. From living on the west side, I knew that when people ask for five or ten dollars, it is often for drugs, so my antennas went up. Another time, he asked me to take him to a friend's house. I did, but he went inside alone and came back out about ten minutes later. I never met the friend, and the building looked rough and unsettling. Sometimes, he also seemed different, like he wasn't himself. Still, he was always respectful to my girls and very sweet to me. He always went to work and dressed nicely. My instincts told me he might have a drug problem, but his actions did not always match what I expected from someone struggling with addiction.

One day, he told me he was coming by after work, and I said okay. It was a nice day, and the girls wanted to be outside. My oldest had a friend over, and we were all sitting on the porch. I saw a guy walking down the street wearing jeans, a wife-beater T-shirt, and a baseball hat tilted to the side. As he got closer, I realized it was Jeremy. I couldn't believe he would come to my house in front of my kids looking like a straight thug. Every other time I had seen him, he looked put together. He had swag, but he never looked like he had just been released from county jail. Even the girls looked embarrassed.

When I asked him why he was dressed like that, he got offended. He said it was hot outside. He was also upset that I told him he looked like a thug. He argued that it was no different from a woman wearing a short skirt or booty shorts because of the heat. I reminded him that I never wore either and told him I did not want him dressing like that around me or my girls again. This became our first argument, and he left my house angry.

About a week after he asked for the ten dollars, I called him to ask when he planned to pay me back. It wasn't that I needed the money, but I wanted to see if he was a man of his word. It was a test of his character, and he failed. He got very upset that I called him about the money and told me he would pay it back but warned me not to disrespect him like that again.

After that, I became convinced that he might have a drug problem. I told myself to leave him alone. He had served his purpose, which was ending my five-year drought, and I didn't have time for drama. I was in the process of finding another apartment, this time in the far western suburbs, far away from the city. I also decided I would not tell him where I was moving. At that point, he could keep the ten dollars. I wished him the best in life. I was done.

Chapter *2*

Discovery:

What is Happening?

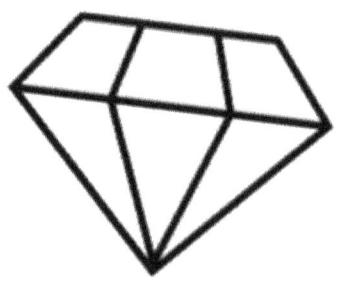

It had been about eight weeks, and I realized I had not gotten my period. The only times in my life I had ever missed my period were when I was pregnant, and that had happened twice. Dear God, please do not let me be pregnant by this guy. I barely knew him, and I suspected he might have a drug problem. No, no, no, this could not be happening. I thought that if I were pregnant, I would not have this baby. No one would ever know, and since I was moving, Jeremy would not be a factor anyway.

I went and bought a pregnancy test, and sure enough, it came back positive. Lawd.

Oh shit, not again. I could not be pregnant by this man. I barely knew him. I could not bring another baby into this world and raise it by myself again. I also did not want to start over. Ashley was now eight years old, and the thought of starting all over again was overwhelming. Bottles, diapers, strollers, daycare. Oh no. I decided I would have an abortion and not tell anyone. That was my plan. I had not heard from Jeremy in over a week, so he did not even have to know. Plus, I was in the process of moving to the suburbs, so he would not know how to contact me anyway. That settled it. I was getting an abortion. I called and made an appointment for Saturday morning. I would tell my sister I needed to work and have her watch the girls.

Saturday morning came, but I could not bring myself to go to the clinic. I did not even take the girls to my sister's house. I told myself I still had a couple of weeks before it was too late, so I would go the following weekend instead. Maybe something would happen, and I would lose the baby naturally. Then I could pretend I never even knew I was pregnant. Lawd, what was everyone going to say about me getting pregnant again without being married? I did not want to deal with people and their comments. The only two people whose opinions truly mattered to me were my big sister and Jasmine. Jasmine was almost fourteen, and I did not want her to think her mother was a hoe who slept with anyone. I had sex with a man I barely knew, and it was unprotected. What was I thinking?

The next Saturday arrived, and once again I sat on the edge of the bed, unable to go. I started praying and told God that if this baby was meant to be, the child's father would find me and we would be together. After that prayer, I made one final appointment at the clinic. This would be the last one. If I did not go, then I would have the baby.

The following week, I was at work when my phone rang at my desk. I answered it, and it was Jeremy. He asked if he could come to my job to talk for a minute. I told him I would meet him at the Starbucks on the corner of Roosevelt and State Street at 12:30 p.m. I also told him that I needed to talk to him as well. I could not believe he was calling after being silent for over a week. Was this a sign from God telling me to keep the baby?

As I approached Starbucks, I saw Jeremy sitting outside, waiting for me. He smiled when he saw me, but he looked a little different. He did not look as put together as he usually did. He stood up, hugged me, and told me I looked nice and that he was happy to see me. I loved his hugs, and I was happy to see him too. We went inside, and I ordered a latte. He said he was fine and did not order anything. We found a table outside so we could talk.

He started by apologizing for disappearing for a couple of weeks. He told me he had been forced to move out of the halfway house after missing curfew one night and that he was now staying at the Salvation Army. He explained that he had to go through detox for a couple of weeks and could not contact anyone. I was shocked and asked, "Detox?" Then I asked, "What are you addicted to?" He told me he was addicted to drugs. I was stunned and terrified at the same time. In my mind, I thought, oh shit, what have I done? I am pregnant by a drug addict. How am I going to handle this and explain it to my family?

Jeremy immediately noticed my expression, grabbed my hand, and reassured me that he wanted to kick the habit. He told me this was not going to be his life. He promised me he would never hurt my girls or me and that I would be safe. I do not know what it was about him, but I felt safe in that moment and believed that he truly wanted to get clean.

Then he asked, "What did you want to talk to me about?" I took a deep breath and blurted it out. I told him I was pregnant. I wanted to see how he would react because his response would help determine what I would do next. He took a deep breath and said okay. Then I told him I was not going to have the baby because I did not want to raise another child alone. He told me I would not be alone and that he would be there with me. I told him I had heard that before and yet here I was, raising two kids on my own. He promised me that if I had the baby, he would be there every step of the way.

I told him I was not looking for his approval and that I was simply informing him. Then I told him I needed to get back to work and that we would talk later. He stood up, hugged me again, and I went back to work.

Later that evening, he called to check on me and told me he enjoyed talking with me. He said he knew I made enough money to do whatever I wanted regarding the baby, but he asked me again to keep it and promised he would be there. I told him I was afraid to take that chance. I was already raising two children by two different fathers. The first man I loved and planned to marry was too focused on being a musician and sleeping with other women. The second was in the army and traveled the world. He sent child support, but that was it. I loved my girls, but I could not do this again. I did not want to do this alone. Both of my parents were deceased, and I did not have much help beyond my two sisters, who had families of their own.

He listened quietly and then said, "Just think about it. Get some rest, and I will talk to you tomorrow."

The next day was Friday, and he called me at work to ask what I was doing after work. I told him I was picking up the girls and that we did not have any plans afterward. He said, "After you pick up the girls, let's all go to the lakefront." I said okay, that sounded good, and I knew the girls would love it.

I picked up the girls and then picked him up. We drove to North Avenue Beach and walked along the lakefront. The girls had fun playing in the sand, and afterward we bought ice cream and sat by the lake watching the water. Then he said again, "Please consider having this baby. I really do not believe in abortions." I told him that I did not either, but I was scared to do this again. It is hard when you do not have help. Once again, he reassured me that I would not be doing this by myself. In that moment, I thought, this guy is different. Then I realized something else. He never asked the question that every other man would have asked, "Is this my baby?"

When I asked him why he never questioned whether the baby was his, he said he believed me. He also said he did not have much to offer me, so why would I lie or try to trap him into being my child's father? I laughed immediately because it was true. At that time, Jeremy did not have much to offer me financially, but he did offer honesty, truth, and consistency. He had been nothing but kind to my kids and me. He stayed in touch and showed me genuine attention. He had also been honest about his drug problem, yet he never tried to take my money or steal from me. There was something different about him, and I truly trusted his intentions.

By then, we had moved to Naperville, away from the west side. I was able to get an apartment in a beautiful complex at a special rate. It was a two-bedroom, two-bath apartment with our own washer and dryer in the unit. It was not as large as the apartment on the west side, but it was nice and quiet. I chose Naperville because of the strong school district, and Jasmine was getting ready to graduate and start high school. I did not want her attending high school in the city.

One morning, I woke up and went to the bathroom. As I wiped, I saw some blood. I immediately became scared that I might be having a miscarriage. Oh Lord, I cannot call anyone because no one knows I am pregnant. I put on a pad, got ready as usual, and took the kids to school. I decided I would stop at the emergency room near their school and get checked out. I planned to call my boss and tell her I would be late.

At the hospital, they were able to see me right away. I told the nurse I was afraid I might be having a miscarriage. She took me back, and they performed an ultrasound. As I watched the screen, I saw the baby inside me, moving around. I could not believe how active the baby was. My heart jumped, and in that moment, I knew I could not go through with an abortion. The nurse explained that I was spotting because my cervix was expanding, which can happen sometimes. She told me the baby looked fine and sent me home.

I felt both thankful and frightened as I left, wondering how this would change my life. How was I going to tell my kids and my sisters that I was pregnant again?

Chapter *3*

Development:
Developing the Mind and
New Options

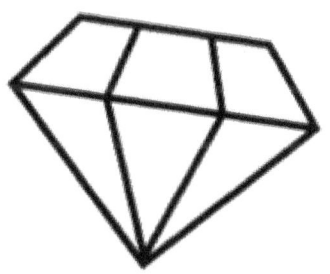

Now that I had decided to keep this baby, I needed to figure out how to tell my daughters and my sister about my decision. Choosing to keep this baby was a huge decision, but after seeing that baby inside me, I knew it was the right one. I prayed that Jeremy would stay by my side and that we could grow into something together. Still, knowing that he struggled with drug addiction scared me deeply.

I went into the girls' bedroom and told them I needed to talk. Jasmine and Ashley sat on the bed, and I sat down next to them. I told them they were going to be big sisters and that I was pregnant. Ashley immediately started jumping up and down, excited. She asked when the baby was coming and began rubbing my belly. Jasmine, on the other hand, looked angry. She stood up and asked, "By who?" When I told her it was Jeremy, she said she needed space and acted like she was going to walk out of the apartment.

I stopped her right away and told her I knew this was a lot to take in, but she was not leaving the house. I explained that she could have time alone to process everything, but the situation was happening regardless. She then asked if I was going to marry Jeremy. I told her I was going to give him an honest opportunity to be part of the baby's life and our lives as well. She stayed in her room for the rest of the day, and I gave her the space she needed.

Telling my oldest daughter was the hardest part, but I knew she would eventually understand. She did not want to see me struggle with raising another child alone.

Telling my sister was not easy either, but at the end of the day, I was a grown woman and did not need her approval. I wanted her support, but the decision was mine. Eventually, I would also have to tell my friends and coworkers, but their opinions did not matter as much.

The next day, I called my sister Denise and told her I was pregnant. The first thing she asked was, "By whom?" I rarely brought men around my kids or my family, so they did not know I had been seeing Jeremy for months. I lived on my own, and my siblings did not really know what I was doing or who I was spending time with. When Jeremy came over and the kids were home, he was strictly introduced as my friend. We would watch movies, sit outside, or talk. When we wanted adult time, it happened when the kids were gone, when we went elsewhere, or even in the car.

My sister told me she would support me, but I could hear the disappointment in her voice. She was upset that I had allowed myself to be in this situation again. The main thing I kept reminding myself was that I was almost finished with my bachelor's degree, and I knew I would be able to take care of my children no matter what.

Jeremy told me he had already prayed and asked God that the next woman he had a child with would be his wife. He already had two sons by two different women. He loved his boys deeply and was a great father to them. They lived in California, but he talked about them often and called them whenever he could. They were always excited to hear from him.

He also loved both of his parents, his mother and his father. Even though they were never married, he stayed in close contact with them. His mother was especially important to him, and he spoke to her almost every day. When he moved back from California, he had hoped to live with her, but she had already relocated to Detroit, Michigan, with her husband. Jeremy was disappointed that she had not told him about the move, but he accepted it and kept moving forward. He also struggled with accepting his mother's marriage to his stepfather.

Once the most important people in my life knew I was pregnant, I felt a sense of relief and could begin planning for the baby. Jeremy and I made our relationship official, and he became my boyfriend. He started coming over more often, and eventually I allowed him to spend the night on weekends. This was a big step for me because I had never allowed a man to stay overnight while my kids were home. Still, I enjoyed having him around as a support system. He fixed things around the house, helped with the girls, and even assisted with homework. He was especially good at math, much better than I was.

At the time, I was working downtown at the law school as the registrar. One day, the bookstore manager asked if I knew anyone looking for a part-time job. He preferred a man because the position required lifting and shelving books. I immediately thought of Jeremy. He went in for the interview dressed professionally, and they hired him on the spot. He ended up working one floor below me. He often brought me lunch or bought me a drink on hot days. He made me feel seen and appreciated. My coworkers loved him, and more than one of them said there was something special about him.

Jeremy was very attentive toward me. He walked me to the train every afternoon after work and made sure no one bumped into me while I was pregnant. We went to lunch on State Street and had fun laughing and talking. We also went out with coworkers after work, and he once told me to introduce him as my fiancée. I told him no way because people would immediately start looking for a ring, and we were not there yet. On the weekends, he caught the train with me and spent time with the girls and me. It did not take long for me to start falling in love with him, especially while carrying his baby.

He made sure to attend my doctor's appointments. I had never had a man go to doctor visits with me before. He rubbed my belly, talked to the baby through my stomach, and sometimes kissed my belly. He was convinced I was having a boy because he said he only had sons. Most of my friends were hoping for a boy as well.

The day of the ultrasound appointment to find out the baby's sex finally arrived, but Jeremy could not attend because he was working at the bookstore. The doctor performed the ultrasound and told me I was having another girl. I asked the doctor to write it down so I could show Jeremy. I went to the bookstore and handed him the envelope with the baby's sex inside. When he saw that it was a girl, his mouth hung open, and he stared in disbelief. I started laughing because he was completely shocked that he had made a little girl. I think it was at that moment he realized he needed to get his life together.

At the time, Jeremy was living at another halfway house in the city. He had to be in by a certain time every night and submit a notice early if he planned to leave for the weekend. Almost every weekend, he spent it with us. He would come out on Fridays and head back on Monday mornings. We always had a great time together, and I truly enjoyed his company.

One day, he called me at work and asked if I was driving that day. I told him yes. He asked if I could pick him up after work, and I said no problem. When I arrived at the halfway house, he had all his belongings packed in a bag, and his friend Tyrone was helping him bring everything to the car. Once I got there, he asked if it would be okay for him to stay with us for a little while until he could get his own place. When I asked what happened, he told me the administration was giving him a hard time and that he had missed curfew, so they asked him to leave.

I was a little skeptical because I had never lived with a man before, and I was unsure how the girls would react to this change. Still, I could not just leave him, and by that point, I had fallen in love with him. I told him we would make it work and figure out the details later. When we got home, I explained to the girls that he would be moving in and that I needed to give this a try for the baby's sake. I also reassured them that I was always there for them and that they could talk to me if they ever felt uncomfortable.

It has been several weeks since Jeremy moved in, and so far, things have been good. We take the train to work and come home together. He helps me cook and even assists the girls with their math homework, which I am terrible at. He is still adjusting to suburban living, though he misses the city. Some Saturdays, he tells me he is going into the city, and I do not hear from him again until the evening. Of course, my first thought is that he is doing something behind my back, but I never have proof. At times, he comes home extremely sleepy, almost nodding off while sitting with me. That is when I started to get suspicious, and I decided to begin paying closer attention to his money.

We discussed and decided that I would pay the rent each month and that he would pay all the utilities. He said no problem, and in the beginning, he did a great job paying those bills. One day, the mail came, and I opened the cable bill to find a disconnect notice. I asked Jeremy about it, and he said, "Don't worry, I will take care of it." After that, he started staying in the city on the nights we got paid, and I began coming home by myself. I didn't allow myself to worry too much because I was about seven months pregnant, and I didn't want stress to send me into labor.

One day, Jeremy's mom called me and said she wanted to be involved in planning a baby shower for me. I was truly surprised because I had never met her in person. She told me she was coming from Michigan for the baby shower and was willing to help pay for it. Of course, I told her she could stay with us, and she said that would be great. When she arrived, we ended up having a wonderful baby shower at the clubhouse of our apartment complex. His family was very excited about the granddaughter who was on the way.

As time went on, the bills were getting paid less consistently, and I was getting closer to my due date. Jeremy never stole anything from me or from the house, but he had started showing patterns of someone who was using drugs again. One day, I sat him down and asked if he was using drugs, and of course, he denied it. I told him that if he could not pay the utility bills, then he would have to leave. We got into a huge argument, and he left that night. I had no idea where he was going, and I didn't hear from him for a couple of days.

One of my friends, who also worked at the bookstore, came to my office and told me she saw him at work and that he looked dirty. I didn't go down there to check because I didn't want to see him like that. Later that day, he caught me as I was leaving work and walked me to the train. He told me he was sorry and that he knew he had disappointed me. I told him that he was disappointed in himself and reminded him that this baby would need her father.

My doctor told me I would be having a C-section and asked if I wanted to have the baby before or after Christmas. I chose to have the baby before Christmas so I could be home for the holiday. The C-section was scheduled for December 20th, which worked perfectly and allowed me to plan ahead. I did all my Christmas shopping for the girls, put up the tree, and completed my grocery shopping early. I spoke with Jeremy, and he told me he would be at the hospital for the delivery. He said he would come over the night before so we could ride to the hospital together. I was so happy just knowing he would be there. I had never had a man in the delivery room with me before.

The night before the surgery, Jeremy never showed up. He called me twice, saying he was on his way, but he never arrived. I was extremely upset and felt sick, worrying that something had happened to him. I had no way to contact him, and I began to lose hope that he would be there for the delivery. We arrived at the hospital, and still no Jeremy. My niece and my sister kept asking where he was, and all I could say was, "I don't know." My heart felt heavy because I couldn't believe he wouldn't show up for this. When the nurse asked if the father was present, I said no. My sister offered to go into surgery with me, but I declined because I truly believed he would still arrive and was just running late.

The nurse came to prepare me for surgery and wheeled me into the operating room. Still no Jeremy. I was already on the table, and the procedure had begun when I saw the surgery door open. A nurse peeked in and told me that the baby's father had arrived and was getting dressed to join me. I felt such relief knowing he was okay and would be there for the birth of his child. When I finally saw him, I could tell he was using drugs again, but in that moment, I was simply grateful he was there.

Jeremy sat next to me during the C-section, holding my hand and rubbing my head the entire time. When the doctors delivered the baby, we heard her cry. The doctor said, "This is a big one." I was lying there in tears. He weighed her and announced that she was 9 pounds, 11 ounces, and 27 inches long. I couldn't believe it. They placed her on my chest, and I began to cry uncontrollably. Jeremy was crying too, and he looked incredibly nervous. After the nurses finished cleaning her up, they handed her to Jeremy. He held his baby girl in his arms and stood off to the side, quietly talking to her. I asked everyone to give him a moment alone with his daughter. To this day, I do not know what he said to her, but I believe he promised to be there for her, and I believe he asked God to take this addiction away from him.

Jeremy had a suitcase in the hallway the entire time he was at the hospital. He left the hospital that day and checked himself into a 17-month treatment program. He told me that he would not be in contact with me for the first 30 days because he had to go through detox. He apologized for leaving at this time, but said he had to do it now or never. I told him I understood, that I loved him, and that we would be here when he finished.

I never thought I would be coming home with my new baby, my two daughters, and no baby daddy again. For all those months, I had Jeremy by my side every step of the way, and now I was alone again. My niece picked me up from the hospital, and as soon as I got in the car, Jasmine started telling me what had happened while I was gone. My niece Kierra had her friends over at my apartment. Kierra was supposed to be watching the girls while I was in the hospital. However, she brought her girlfriend over to spend the night, and Jasmine was not having anyone disrespect our home. Jasmine confronted Kierra, and they got into an argument. Kierra said that Jasmine pulled a knife on her and told her she was not afraid to use it if she didn't get her girlfriend out of our house. I was proud of Jasmine for standing up for our home, but she should not have threatened anyone with a knife. Still, this was the last thing I wanted to deal with while coming home with a newborn and stitches.

I am on maternity leave for three months. I am also still taking classes online, which has not been easy while nursing a baby. The girls enjoy having me home every day and love spending time together. Jeremy has not called in a few weeks, so I am missing him and hoping he is okay. In the meantime, motherhood continues.

Jasmine and Ashley keep me busy, along with my new bundle of joy, Tabatha. Tabatha is the happiest little chubby-faced baby you could meet. She is already sleeping four hours at a time and smiling. We have completely fallen in love with her. Jasmine was not happy about me being pregnant again, but she has already become the best big sister. Ashley thinks Tabatha is her baby doll. She always wants to hold her and loves taking naps with her. I feel so blessed watching my three girls, and I am incredibly grateful that God gave them to me, despite their fathers.

Jasmine's dad was a musician, a saxophone player in many bands. I loved him deeply and truly believed we would get married one day. The problem was that several other women believed the same thing. He was six-foot-three with a muscular build. When I went to watch him play, there would be tables full of women screaming and calling his name. He always told me they were just groupies, but I knew some of them were more than that.

I later found out that two other women were pregnant at the same time I was pregnant with Jasmine. We broke up a long time ago, and I am so grateful I dodged that bullet.

Ashley's dad was tall, slender, and very dark chocolate. He was smart and a bit of a nerd. He was a good friend of my best friend Paula's boyfriend at the time. We would all hang out at Paula's house, play cards, drink, and just kick it. One day, Charlie, Ashley's dad, asked if I could give him a ride home. I was happy to do so because we were all friends. Needless to say, we started dating shortly after that ride. Things were good until he enlisted in the Army. Soon after he enlisted, I found out I was pregnant with Ashley. He never denied Ashley, but he became caught up in enjoying his life and never truly came back around to be a dad. He sent child support, but that was about it.

I took both men to court for child support because Lord knows I needed the money. Jasmine's dad, Joseph, kept coming to court with excuse after excuse as to why he could not pay. He never held a job long enough for child support to be deducted from his paycheck. The only money I ever received from him came when he was arrested for past-due support and the court sent me the money he posted for bail. At one point, I told him he did not need to pay support, but that he should at least be available to help watch the kids when I needed him. He did that for about a month, then returned to his old ways. I even helped him get a job, but he only kept it for about a month before being fired. He could never hold a job because he stayed out late playing in bands at clubs.

Ashley's dad, Charley, paid child support the entire time he was in the Army, which was a huge help. I received it for about four years like clockwork. Then, all of a sudden, it stopped coming in, and I had to go back to court. That is when I found out he had left the Army and was currently unemployed. I reached out to him, and he asked if he could come over to see Ashley and talk. I told him sure, it was no problem.

He came over and sat on the couch with Ashley for a while. We made small talk, but he barely interacted with her. It was getting late, so I told Ashley to get ready for bed. I then walked him to the door. As he was leaving, he whispered in my ear that he was hoping he could stay over to be with me. I looked at him in disgust and told him to get out. I also told him he never needed to come back if that was his intention. That was the last time we ever saw Charley, and to this day, Ashley does not know what that man even looks like.

After dealing with all the mess involving these two fathers, I prayed and asked God to bless me so I would never again have to ask these men to take care of their children. I also asked God to bless me with a man who would love my children like they were his own and love them unconditionally. I asked God to send me a man who loved his momma, because a man who loves his momma would love me as well. Finally, I asked for a man who already had children and truly enjoyed being a dad. I figured that if he already had kids, he would know how to handle mine too. I had dated men without children before, and they did not have the patience my girls required.

Eventually, I received a call from Jeremy letting me know he had finished the detox portion of his recovery program. He was in good spirits and eager to come over and see all of us, especially his baby. He told me he would catch the train to my apartment and spend the whole day with us. Since he was still in the recovery program, he was not allowed to stay overnight yet. He arrived on the first train the next morning, and we spent the entire day together. I cooked breakfast and dinner, we watched movies, and he bonded with his baby.

For the next few months, Jeremy came over whenever he had a free day to spend with us. Sometimes he stopped by my job to bring me something to drink or met me for lunch. He invited all of us to go to church with him one Sunday. They were having a family day, and lunch was served after the service. He proudly introduced us to everyone as his family and always referred to my oldest daughter as his daughter. That meant so much to me and made me truly feel like we were becoming a family.

Even though things felt good, in the back of my mind I struggled with the fact that I was in love with a drug addict. Most people had no idea what we were going through, and Jeremy did not fit the image people associate with addiction. He was always well dressed, polite, hardworking, and attractive. He never stole from anyone and never hurt anyone but himself. He truly was his own worst enemy.

About six months into the treatment program, Jeremy decided he wanted to be with us more than he wanted to remain in the program. In my selfish thoughts, I wanted him home with us too. I believed he no longer needed the program at that point. I told him it would be fine if he left and came to live with us. I wanted that family feeling, and I wanted help with the kids. I knew he would find a job and contribute because that is the kind of person he is. He always wanted to make sure we were taken care of.

He left the program and moved in with us. Within a week, he secured a job at Target on the overnight stock team. He chose that job because he did not have a car and could walk to work from the apartment. I was proud of him, and things were going well with us living together again.

After about a month of Jeremy living with us again and adjusting to life with a new baby, I realized that the two-bedroom apartment was no longer big enough. I started looking for a place to rent with at least three bedrooms. We found a townhome and moved in right before Thanksgiving. Jeremy's dad, brother, and stepmom all came to help us move. We were so excited. Both older girls got their own rooms. Ashley would eventually share with Tabatha, but for now, the baby stayed in the room with us.

We truly started living like a family, and I loved every moment of it. Jeremy even got a car and a better job working for a lawn care company. In my mind, we were finally living the American dream. However, you can take the man out of the city, but you cannot take the city out of the man.

Chapter *4*

Digging:

Looking Deeper to Find Answers!

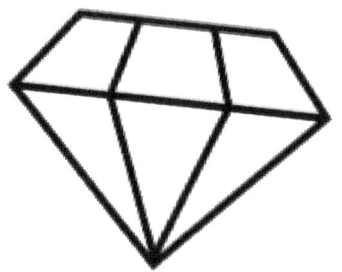

Jeremy was still a Southsider at heart, and he was always thinking of ways to make money. He began selling gym shoes on the side to make extra cash. Soon, instead of spending weekends with us, he started driving to the city to sell shoes out of his car, at barber shops, and in various other places. I hated going to the city every weekend, and my insecurities were through the roof. I was not as worried about him seeing other women as I was about him possibly using drugs again. He had been clean for a year, and I did not believe our relationship would survive if he started using again.

One Saturday, I told Jeremy he needed to be home in time for me to get my hair done so he could watch the baby. He came home at the last minute, and something felt off about him. I went ahead and got ready to leave, but I told Ashley to help watch Tabatha and to call me if she needed anything. Jeremy was very agitated and kept moving and nodding at the same time. I felt nervous about leaving, but I knew he would never do anything to hurt the girls.

Ashley called me a couple of times, telling me he was acting strange and that she had brought Tabatha into the room with her. I reassured her that she was doing a great job and told her I was on my way home. When I arrived, Jeremy was asleep. When I asked him about his behavior earlier, he claimed he had no idea what I was talking about. From that moment on, I paid close attention and watched him like a hawk.

Over the next few weeks, I observed his behavior more carefully. I noticed signs that made it seem like he might be using again, but I could not confirm it for sure. I told myself I would wait and see what happened when he got paid and whether he had money for the bills. With Jeremy, that was always the clearest indicator. As I mentioned before, he had never stolen from anyone, which is not typical behavior for someone actively using.

Payday arrived, and when he got home, I told him how much money I needed for bills and groceries. He immediately became angry and started arguing with me about money. He then began making excuses for not having any. At that moment, I knew he was using again, because money had never been an issue before. We got into a huge argument, and I told him I was not willing to put up with him using drugs and contributing nothing financially. I refused to do this alone and told him he had to leave. He said, "No problem, I will leave," and walked out, slamming the door behind him.

I was devastated because we were supposed to leave the following week for a work trip. He was originally going with us, but I knew that was no longer an option now that I believed he was using again. I called the landlord and asked him to change the locks. I lied and said we had lost our keys and that I was worried someone else might have them. He came over that same day and changed all the locks. I did not believe Jeremy would hurt us, but I wanted to make sure the house was secure while we were out of town.

I did my best to hide my emotions during the trip, but I was still deeply hurt and disappointed. I told myself to push those feelings aside and enjoy Disneyland with the girls. The trip was for a work conference, but I often planned these trips around the girls' spring break. My job covered the hotel room, and I paid for their plane tickets. Jasmine was old enough to stay with the younger girls in the room while I attended conference sessions. Afterward, I would pick them up and spend the rest of the day at the park. We always had a great time, and Ashley still says those were the best trips of her life.

On the last day of the trip, my thoughts returned to Jeremy. I had no idea where he was or where he was sleeping. I prayed that he was okay. Regardless of everything, he was still the father of my child. I did not want anything bad to happen to him, but I also knew I had to stand firm. He could not live with us and use drugs. He had to make a choice.

As soon as I returned home, the phone rang, and it was Jeremy. He sounded sweet and immediately apologized for his behavior. He also expressed that he did not like being kicked out, having the locks changed, and then being left behind while we went out of town. I listened, but I stood firm in my reasons. He did not tell me where he was staying, which made me anxious. He did say he was still going to work, and that gave me some reassurance. I could not help but wonder if he was staying with another woman, but I did not ask.

Two weeks passed, and he was still out of the house. One day, he called and asked if I would take him to pick up his paycheck. I was confused because he had a car. He told me the car broke down and that when he went back to where it was parked, it was gone. It had either been stolen or towed, and he had no idea which. I agreed to take him to get his check. He took the train to the house, and I drove him to his job.

When he opened the envelope, it was not a paycheck at all. It was a deposit slip. His pay had already been deposited into his bank account, and his account was overdrawn from writing bad checks to get money.

When he realized that the envelope did not contain a check, he looked completely defeated. He already appeared as though he had been sleeping in his car, and when I finally asked him, he admitted that he had been. I felt sorry for him, so I asked if he wanted to come to the house to eat and get some rest. He said yes, so we went back to the house.

As soon as Tabatha saw her daddy, she smiled and gave him a big hug. She kept playing with him, and he got down on the floor to play with her and Ashley as well. Jasmine looked upset that he was back in the house, but I ignored it, knowing she was a teenager.

I let him take a shower and fixed him some food. Before I knew it, he was asleep. He fell asleep right there on the living room floor. I left him there and covered him with a blanket. He looked exhausted and pitiful. My mom always told me to feed someone when they were hungry, and that was what I felt I was doing. This man was not just anyone, and I loved him despite everything.

The next morning, he asked if he could ride into the city with me. I told him sure, it was no problem. As we were driving, he asked if I would drop him off at another drug rehabilitation center. He explained that this would be his last attempt. He told me we would have to break up so he could fully commit to the program and complete it this time. He said he needed to do this not only for himself but for his family as well.

I did not fully understand why we had to break up, but he told me it was part of his recovery process. I told him okay. He got out of the car that day, and I did not hear from him again for another 30 days.

Chapter *5*

Sifting Soil:

Working Through Stuff

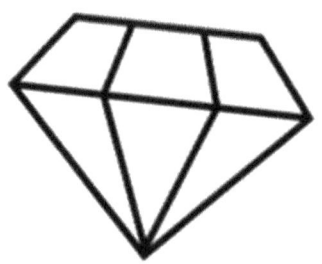

Jeremy completed the detox portion of the program and now has a sponsor. He cannot spend the night yet, but he does have movement during the day. He found a job working at a collection company, which allows him to go to work and then return to the rehabilitation facility. He is actively involved in his meetings, and they often have retreats and events for people in the program. He has earned a good reputation for being hardworking, dependable, and a leader among the men.

We are technically not dating anymore, but he calls me whenever he gets the chance, and I am being supportive during this time. He also checks on the girls regularly.

I am so proud of Jeremy. He is committed to his program, meets with his sponsor, Reggie, consistently, and continues to work. He now comes over to spend time with us on the weekends, and we are back together. He is great with the kids and is learning what it means to be a father to a ready-made family. Jasmine sometimes gives him a lot of attitude. She is not used to having a man in the house, and she shows it.

In addition to supporting Jeremy, I am preparing to graduate with my bachelor's degree in communications. It took me seven years to complete this degree because I worked full-time while attending school part-time. My family was proud, and I was extremely proud of myself. Becoming a college graduate had always been a dream of mine, and it was finally happening. My family, friends, coworkers, and yes, Jeremy, were all present at the graduation ceremony. Afterward, we went out to eat to celebrate. My next goal is to pursue my master's degree.

Seeing me graduate seemed to motivate Jeremy. He decided to earn his GED and enrolled in a program with his friend Tyrone. They completed the program and graduated together. I was so proud of them. I took Jeremy's diploma, framed it, and made sure he hung it on the wall. I wanted him to understand that every step forward is an accomplishment.

Jeremy completed the full 17-month rehabilitation program and graduated with honors. During that time, he became a leader, developed a strong bond with his sponsor, Reggie, and followed all the steps of the program. He attends Narcotics Anonymous meetings regularly and continues working the 12 steps. He addressed past pain related to his father and apologized to those he hurt during his addiction. He has grown tremendously and is now ready to live a life free from addiction. We are officially living together and continuing to blend our families.

Jasmine is now about 17 years old and very much a teenager. She is great with her sisters, but she has been acting up at school. She is extremely smart, but she gets bored and loses interest. During parent-teacher conferences, I was told that when she completes her homework, she earns all A's, but when she does not turn it in, she receives F's. It was frustrating as a parent because I knew she could achieve anything if she applied herself.

One day, I came home from work to find Jasmine upset because Jeremy had told her that her friends could not come over and be loud or disrespectful in the house. She raised her voice at him and then went to her room and slammed the door. I told Jasmine that she needed to respect him as the man of the house and understand that he was not going anywhere. She rolled her eyes and stayed in her room.

Ashley, on the other hand, was mostly happy having Jeremy as her dad. She felt protected and cared for. Jeremy took Ashley to her first father-daughter dance, and I was so thankful she finally had that experience. I made sure he brought her flowers. Jeremy wore a suit, and they sent me pictures of them dancing together. Seeing those photos filled my heart with joy.

Ashley would often ask Jeremy for things, and he always did his best to make her happy. She asked him for a pair of Air Force One gym shoes with her name airbrushed on the side. About a week later, he surprised her with the shoes. She was the only girl at school with her name on her sneakers. Spoiled.

Jeremy would often go above and beyond for the girls and always acknowledged them as his children, even when they gave him attitude or acted like they did not want to be bothered by him. He is exactly what I prayed for. I often prayed that God would send me a man who would love my family the way my father loved ours.

My dad met my mother here in Chicago. At that time, her children were living in Mississippi with my grandmother while my mom worked in Chicago to earn money. After my parents married, my dad told my mom they needed to bring the children to Chicago so they could be a family. My dad drove to Mississippi, brought all my siblings back, and we became one household. When my mom became pregnant with me, my dad raised all of us together as one family. He never referred to anyone as a stepchild or himself as a stepdad. He used to say that the only step was the one you took when you walked into the house.

I feel like Jeremy is just like my dad and exactly what I prayed for. That is when I realized he was everything I wanted in a partner and that God had already blessed me, even though I did not see it at first. I think I did not recognize it because he did not arrive in a perfect package. He came a little rough and needed some polishing, but his core was strong and ready to shine. He truly was a diamond in the rough.

Jeremy and I decided to buy Jasmine a used car when she got her first job working at Jewel. Jeremy was the one who took her out every day and taught her how to drive. I did not have the patience to teach her, and she said Jeremy was much calmer than I was. We found an older Toyota Camry and bought it for two thousand dollars. Jasmine was thrilled, but she was only allowed to drive it to school and work.

About two months later, we discovered that Jasmine was leaving the house each morning but returning after we went to work and sleeping instead of going to school. I found out she had been missing a lot of classes and would not graduate on time. She needed an additional credit to graduate. I was so disappointed and tried everything I could to help her finish, but she had started hanging out with kids who were a bad influence.

One day, I came home from work and found that she had moved out. Her closet was empty, and all her clothes were gone. I called her and told her that since she was now 18, she could make her own choices, but she had until midnight to return the car or we would report it stolen. She parked the car at the train station and told me I could pick it up there. Jeremy drove me to the station, and we brought the car home. We later sold it to teach her a lesson.

That was the beginning of Jasmine truly testing my patience for a while. I thank God for Jeremy and his support during that difficult time.

Chapter *6*

Looking for the Shiny Object: What About a Ring?

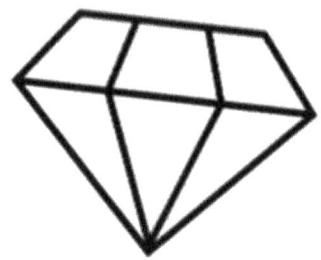

Jeremy was able to get himself a county job. He was hired as a water meter reader for the county. He was responsible for going around and reading water meters for county homeowners. He was very proud of this position because it was a career job. It offered many opportunities for growth, and he looked forward to moving up within the department. The job also paid well, so he was excited to finally make decent money.

This job was perfect for Jeremy because it allowed him to work independently and alongside a diverse group of men. He was the only Black man on the team, which was new for him. Most of the guys were fine to work with, but there were a couple who were openly prejudiced. Jeremy had to learn how to deal with difficult people without letting his South Side instincts take over when problems arose. I told him this was another step in his growth as a man. Sometimes we have to choose our battles and think about the consequences of our actions.

That advice paid off because Jeremy took his frustration and turned it into motivation. He began studying for his wastewater license. He learned that earning this license would allow him to make more money and open more doors for advancement. He came home every day and studied for hours in the bedroom. The exam was very challenging, but when he finally took it, he passed on the first try. Once again, I was extremely proud of him. When a position opened up, he applied and was hired as a wastewater operator for the county. Jeremy was proud of himself, and I was proud of him too.

At this point, we were living what felt like the American dream. Jeremy had a solid county job and had been clean for a couple of years. Tabatha was growing fast and attending daycare. Ashley was doing great, playing the clarinet in the school band and enjoying being a kid. Jasmine was living in the city with friends. We were not happy about her living situation, but we remained supportive. We lived in a nice little townhouse in a great neighborhood and looked like a suburban middle-class family.

However, we were not married, and I started to notice that marriage had not even been a serious topic of discussion. Every time I brought it up, Jeremy would say, "It will happen, just give it some time." By now, we had been together on and off for almost four years.

Christmas was coming, and it was shaping up to be a good one for all of us. Jeremy's mom came to spend Christmas with us and to celebrate Tabatha's birthday. Their birthdays were close together, so we celebrated both the holiday and her birthday at the same time. We bought the kids lots of presents and woke up early on Christmas morning to open gifts. We all wore matching Christmas pajamas, and Jeremy spent the morning putting toys together. I went into the kitchen to make breakfast, and later that day we went to my family's house for Christmas dinner.

It was a wonderful day, and we truly looked like the perfect American family. Still, deep down, I felt like it was time for us to make things official.

New Year's Eve, we were at the house with Jeremy, the kids, and his mom, and we started talking about our New Year's resolutions and goals for the coming year. When it was Jeremy's turn, he talked about getting his CDL and continuing to move forward in his career. His mom shared her goals, and then I talked about mine. After dinner, I realized that Jeremy had not mentioned getting engaged or marriage as a goal for the new year. I could not stop thinking about it, and I even lost sleep over it.

The next morning, as soon as he rolled over, I asked him why he did not mention getting engaged in the upcoming year. He told me flat out that it was not on his schedule for the next year. He said he was not saying never, just not right now. I immediately felt rejected and started crying. I told him it had been almost four years since we met and that I had stood by him through so much. I told him I was no longer willing to keep playing house and that whatever we did in the future, I wanted us to move forward together. He told me he was not ready yet and that he needed to get his finances and career in order first.

I told him that was fine, but if we were not getting married, he needed to be out of the townhouse by the end of January. He said okay, and that was it.

Almost three weeks passed, and Jeremy did not bring up getting engaged, our conversation, or anything at all. I assumed this was the end and that he would be moving out at the end of the month. I began preparing myself mentally for the end of the relationship. My birthday was coming up, and he asked me out to dinner. We went to

Outback Steakhouse and started talking about marriage again. He explained all the reasons he still felt unready, with finances being the main one. I told him I would stand by him regardless and that marriage is about sticking things out together.

By the end of dinner, I thought the conversation was over, and he got up to go to the bathroom. When he returned, he stood beside me, got down on one knee, and pulled a small box out of his pocket. He asked me if I would marry him, and I could not believe it was finally happening. Of course, I said yes. I put on my ring with so much pride and joy. I could not believe we were finally getting married.

Chapter 7

4 Cs of a Diamond:
Cut, Color, Clarity & Carat
I finally Got the Ring!

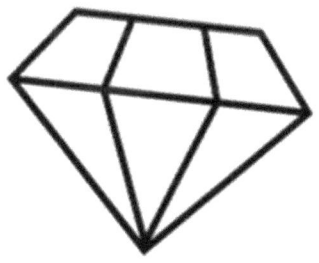

I couldn't wait to go to work on Monday and show off my engagement ring. Jeremy bought what he could afford, but it was still beautiful to me. It was a small solitaire, about a half-carat total. This was okay with me because I believe I will get something bigger the longer we stay together. I was surprised he picked it out all by himself. He did tell my best friend, Desiree, about the ring, and she is the one who told him he must propose and make it special. She told him that every girl wants to have her ring on when she tells everyone that she is engaged. I am so happy he took her advice.

Now it is time to start planning the wedding. I know that I want a sit-down dinner at a banquet hall. I also want our children to attend our wedding, and I want my brother-in-law to marry us because he is an ordained pastor. I have no idea how we are going to pay for this, but I am trusting God that it will be done. We decided the wedding would be in March of next year, and we chose March because we met, started dating, and conceived in March, so we decided that March is the month for all good things.

Jeremy has really stepped it up, and he is becoming the man I didn't know was inside of him. He is a hard worker; he goes to work every day and comes home to take care of the grass and the house. He is a protector, and he doesn't allow his friends to come to the house because he feels his home is his sanctuary, and he is selective about whom he lets into it. That is because when he is with you, he is truly with you, and if you do anything to make him lose his trust, he is done.

Chapter *8*

Deep Excavation:
Learning Everything About
the Families

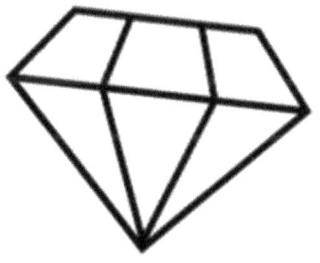

One day, Jeremy's dad called me and asked what my last name would be if we got married. I was confused by the question because he had asked me this before, when I was in the hospital giving birth to Tabatha. At that time, he wanted to know what Tabatha's last name would be. He explained that it was very important to keep the father's last name in the bloodline.

Jeremy's dad was an old Black Panther, and he still had a lot of issues of his own. Jeremy loved his dad, but he did not trust him with his heart or with the kids' hearts. Jeremy's dad had never truly been a dad to him unless Jeremy was in trouble. He was the type of dad who would say he was going to do something and then not show up on that day or at that event. He would also do more for his other kids before doing anything for Jeremy. However, Jeremy looked just like his dad, Big Jeremy. Yes, Jeremy was named after his father, so he is a junior. Then we had little Jeremy, or Jeremy III, but we just called him JJ, short for Jeremy Jr. Jeremy did not use Big Jeremy's last name, so he was still able to give Jeremy III that name.

Mrs. Tonya, Jeremy's mom, told me the story of why Jeremy no longer uses his dad's last name, Thomas. She said she changed Jeremy's last name to her maiden name when he was in the fourth grade. She explained that Big Jeremy never did anything for Jeremy, and she had to do everything for him by herself while also raising another son, Monteal. Big Jeremy was married to another woman named Janet, and they had two boys and a daughter together.

Jeremy uses the last name Jones, not Thomas. Jones is his mom Tonya's maiden name, and this is the name she began using for him when he was in the fourth grade. She registered him for school under Jones, and Jeremy simply got used to it. He gave all his kids the last name Jones, including Tabatha. Therefore, when we get married, our last name will officially be Jones, not Thomas. Big Jeremy did not like this, and he made that very clear to me over the phone.

As we were planning the wedding, I really started missing my parents. Both of my parents are deceased, and I only have my siblings. I have two sisters and a brother. Denise is the oldest sister, and she is like a mother to me. I always strive to make her proud of me, and she is my main support system. Then there is my sister Margaret. She is only eleven months younger than Denise, but she has always been the one who hangs out with me and makes me laugh. She is also a great support system, but only after you have exhausted all other resources do you call Margaret. Lastly, there is my brother Jeremiah. He is the youngest, and he has struggled with substance and alcohol abuse for a long time. However, Jeremiah is the funniest and nicest guy you will ever meet. He loves his family, and women love them some Jeremiah. He always seems to have three or four women taking care of him.

My brother Jeremiah lives downstate in Illinois, and I love it when we all get together for a visit or drive to Peoria to see our elderly uncle. Uncle Smokey is my mom's only living sibling, so we make it a point to visit him together. We have so much fun, and I cherish those moments with my siblings. I am going to have my brother Jeremiah and my uncle Smokey give me away at the wedding, since my dad is not here to do the honors. I couldn't decide between the two, so I decided to have them both.

Jasmine is going to be my maid of honor, and Ashley will be the bridesmaid. Tabatha is the flower girl, and JJ will be the ring bearer. Justin, our oldest son, will be a groomsman, and then Jeremy's sponsor, Reggie, will be his best man. Having our kids as our wedding party makes life much easier for us. We do not have to deal with everyone's opinions because we can simply tell them what we are doing, and that is it. However, having my daughters as part of the wedding party made planning a bachelorette party a little difficult. I am so thankful that my girlfriends stepped in and told Jasmine to allow them to plan the event.

My friend Paula from high school, Destiny from graduate school, and Shanice, one of my friends from the law school where I currently work, all took the initiative to plan and pay for my bachelorette party. They knew Jasmine could not afford it and should not attend a bachelorette party since she was still a teenager, but they wanted to make sure I had a proper celebration. I told them that I did not want any strippers to come to the hotel room we were staying in, but I was okay with going to a strip club, so that is what we decided to do.

We went to the strip club, and it was so much fun. They pulled me onto the stage and danced for me. I had on all the bachelorette accessories, like the sash and the crown. The staff at the club made sure we had a great time, and it turned into an unforgettable night. After the club, we went back to the room, got extremely drunk, and just had a fantastic time talking trash and laughing. The bachelorette party was a huge success and exactly what I wanted for that night.

Chapter *9*

Milling:

The wedding and coming together as a family

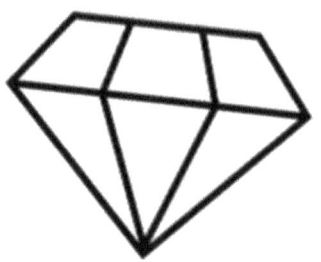

Now it is the week of the wedding, and I am so excited to get this over with. Jeremy is also running around like crazy. The boys' flights arrived, and we had to pick them up from the airport. This would be my first time meeting them in person. We ordered their tuxedos at the store, but we had to wait until they arrived to get them fitted.

The youngest son could not make it because his mother said no. She did not want him to fly unattended. So, Justin and Jeremy Jr. arrived at O'Hare, and Jeremy was so excited to have the boys here. Justin was tall and had a killer smile, and Jeremy Jr. was so sweet and mild-tempered. And then you could tell that he loved his daddy and was just happy to be in his presence. Jeremy immediately took them to get haircuts and buy them some new clothes. You could tell their mom had just thrown their clothes in a suitcase and put them on a plane. The boys looked like they hadn't had their hair cut in months.

Jeremy's mom also came to town. After she arrived, her best friend, Aretha, called and asked if she could stay with us for the wedding. I was so irritated by Aretha because our home was already full, and I did not have anywhere for her to stay. We did not want to be rude, so we allowed her to sleep on the couch downstairs. Tonya, Jeremy's mom, was great. She helped with the kids and helped me around the house. We had our rehearsal and dinner scheduled for that Thursday before the wedding, and the wedding was scheduled for that Saturday afternoon.

We all arrived at the banquet hall for the rehearsal, and everything went very well. We decided to have our rehearsal dinner at Old Country Buffet so everyone could eat whatever they wanted. We were also trying to save money because we were going broke planning this wedding. On our way from the rehearsal, Jeremy got pulled over by the police. They ran his license and found that he was driving without insurance.

Jeremy had the boys in the car, along with his best man, Reggie. Jeremy Jr. was hysterically crying after seeing his dad being arrested. The officers told Reggie to drive the car, and they took Jeremy to jail.

When Reggie arrived at Old Country Buffet, he told me that Jeremy had been arrested and taken to the police station. I became hysterical and extremely worried about my sweetie. Everyone offered to go with me to the police station, but I declined because I needed to pray. Also, when I am focused on something, I need quiet. I told everyone to stay and enjoy the food. I paid the bill for everyone and told them I would be back. If I was not back by the time they finished eating, I instructed my sisters to get the kids home, and we would be back soon.

By the time I arrived at the police station, they had finished booking him. I paid the fine, and they told me he would be released and would need to show proof of insurance by his court date. Praise God, he was released in less than an hour. We were able to get back to the restaurant and enjoy what was left of the rehearsal dinner. We were both frustrated about having to pay that fine, especially with so many final wedding payments due, but somehow, we knew we would be okay.

A Diamond In The Rough: A Love Story

The day of the wedding was very peaceful. Jeremy and I woke up like usual. We did not spend the night apart because we did not want to waste money on hotel rooms. Tonya woke up and decided to make breakfast for us, and she brought it to us in bed, which was extremely nice. She also made breakfast for the whole family. Jeremy and I ate our food and then watched a movie while waiting for it to be time to get ready.

Jeremy and the boys left the house first because Justin's pants did not fit, so they had to stop by the tuxedo shop before heading to the banquet hall. Tonya and the girls also left the house and headed to the banquet hall so they would be there on time. I asked my sister Denise to arrive early and instruct the hostesses on where to stand and how to hand out the seating arrangements. I was at the house by myself, which was great, and I asked my friend Shanice to meet me there and drive me to the venue so we could save money on a limo.

We arrived at the venue, and everything was ready to get started. The photographer took some pictures before the ceremony, and then the wedding began. It was a beautiful ceremony, and everything went just as planned. We had so much fun. We danced, ate well, and truly enjoyed being surrounded by our family and friends. I personally missed my parents not being there physically, but I know they were there in spirit. Jeremy looked so handsome, and I felt a deep sense of peace, which confirmed that he is my soulmate.

After the wedding, we headed to the Sybaris for an overnight stay and some time away from our full house.

On the way to the hotel, we stopped at the store because we were starving. On your wedding day, you do not really get to enjoy the food like your guests do. I barely ate anything because you are too busy smiling, kissing, and taking pictures. You only taste the cake when you cut it for photos. So, on the way to the room, we stopped for snacks.

Once we got to the room, we took off our wedding clothes and sat in the middle of the bed, eating snacks and opening envelopes to read the cards and see how much money we received from the guests. We laughed and talked about the night. We drank some champagne and took a dip in the hot tub in our room. We then spent the rest of the night consummating our marriage. I believe consummation is more intimate than simply having sex. I felt more connected to my husband than I ever had with any of my past boyfriends.

We asked for a late checkout for our one-night stay, and when we checked out, we went straight back home. We could not take a longer honeymoon because we still had kids in town, and Jeremy's mom and her friend were still visiting. We needed to make sure everyone got on their planes and trains to return home. Our house was back to normal about three days after the wedding.

Chapter *10*

Scratching with Sandpaper:

Dealing with the Itches of Blending a Family

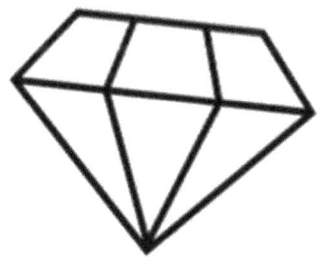

A Diamond In The Rough: A Love Story

Well, now it has been almost a year since we got married, and I am anxious for us to buy our own home. We are still renting the townhouse, and it is okay, but I really want our own place. It has started to consume me, and I spend every waking moment looking for a home. I did not open any of our wedding gifts because I purposely put items on our wedding registry that I wanted for our new home. So I left all those gifts in their boxes until we got home. We walked past the boxes every day, which motivated us to strive for homeownership.

We finally sat down with a home lender and were able to get approval for a home-buying loan. Then we found a realtor that we both liked, and now we could start looking for a home with confidence. Jeremy really wants a house with a basement, but unfortunately, in the western suburbs where we live, there aren't many homes with basements. When you do find one, they usually cost more than what we were approved for. In addition, we probably should look for a house with four bedrooms, but those houses also cost more than our approved amount. Plus, it is only Ashley and Tabatha at home, so three bedrooms are enough.

Jasmine no longer lives with us. She has moved into an apartment with her girlfriend, Courtney. Yes, you heard me: she considers herself gay now. Courtney is a nice girl, and she even attended the wedding. We have no problem with Jasmine being gay, but I don't think she is. I think she is just going through a phase, and eventually, she will leave this lifestyle behind. For some reason, all my nieces, cousins, and my daughter are calling themselves gay. We will see what happens in a few years.

A Diamond In The Rough: A Love Story

We only need three bedrooms and two bathrooms at home. I would like a basement, but I am okay with just a nice-sized family room. We looked at a lot of houses and got outbid on two that we really liked. One of them had a basement, and Jeremy was disappointed that we got outbid on that one. Finally, I found a house that is in the girls' school district and within our price range. We went to see it, and I fell in love with how the sunlight came into the dining room. It does not have a basement, but it does have a big family room and a nice-sized master bedroom with a master bathroom. We put in our bid on this house, and it was accepted. Yay, we are buying a house!

We went through the home-buying process and are getting ready to close on our house. The closing date is scheduled for March 31st, and I thought this was designed by God as well, because everything we have done so far has happened in March. We met in March; we conceived Tabatha in March. We got married in March, and now we are closing on our house on the last day of March. Needless to say, March is our blessed month.

We are moving into our new home, and Jeremy asked Tyrone to come over and help him move. They moved all the furniture in, and the girls were so excited to have their own rooms. Tabatha got her own room for the first time, and I made sure to decorate it with everything Barney. She loved watching Barney, so we bought her sheets, comforters, curtains, towels—everything Barney. They also had their own bathroom, so I made sure it was completely girly with pink and lavender colors. Ashley's room was pink, of course, and we bought her a white bedroom set. She loved her room, and you would often hear her say, "Get out of my room." I love hearing that, and I finally believe that we have made it.

Jeremy was excited to tell everyone that we are homeowners. He went and bought everything to make sure his yard looks good every day. He also bought items for the backyard because he loves sitting out there. He enjoys barbecuing, so he got his yard ready for the summertime in Chicago. I was just happy to be in our own home and to see my kids go out to the backyard and play. The kitchen has a window over the sink, and it makes me proud to look out and see Tabatha playing in the yard. Now, of course, the next step is getting a dog.

One Sunday, we decided to visit the dog shelters to see if they had any puppies we might be interested in adopting. I really wanted a small dog, but Jeremy wanted a big dog, one to protect the family and house. I was a little nervous about a big dog, but maybe if we got it as a puppy, it would be okay. We went to this shelter, and they had just received four mixed-breed puppies. They were Labradors mixed with pit bulls. Jeremy and the girls fell in love with one of the dogs and inquired about adoption. We went through the adoption process and came home two weeks later with our first family dog. We named him Maximus, aka Max.

Max and Tabatha instantly became best buddies. She loved that dog so much, and it is one of the things that started her talking. She had been having problems with speech, and she was going to the speech specialist at school twice a week. However, when we brought Max home from the shelter, her teacher called us and said that for the first time, Tabatha came to school and raised her hand to tell the whole class that she got a new puppy, and his name was Max. This made us so happy, and again, it confirmed that this was a good move. Max immediately became her best friend, and they were inseparable.

Well, now more than ever, we were living the American Dream. We were a two-parent household, two incomes, two cars, and two kids living at home. Our oldest daughter was living on her own, and we could visit her whenever we liked. We were living in the suburbs, and the kids were attending great schools. Ashley was in the show choir at the high school, and we attended all the suburban school events. This was the American Dream, and we had finally arrived.

Then we got a phone call one day from Justin and JJ's mom, Laura. She told Jeremy that she had been really stressed out with the boys. She said that Justin had been kicked out of another junior high school and that she was at her wits' end dealing with them. She said she wasn't working and that, financially, she was struggling. She asked if the boys could come and stay with us for a couple of weeks so she could have a break. It was summertime, and we thought for sure this wouldn't be a big deal.

I was a little frustrated because we had just gotten the house set up, and the girls were beginning to enjoy their new bedrooms. We didn't have another guest bedroom, so one of the girls would have to give up her room for the boys to sleep. In addition, Tabatha only had a twin-size bed, so we would need to buy another twin-size bed to accommodate the boys. Then I said to myself, "This is okay, since it will only be for a couple of weeks. We can make it work."

When the boys arrived, I was taken aback again. Laura had sent them on the plane with a suitcase full of ragged clothes, mismatched socks, and hair that hadn't been cut in a long time. The boys looked like some homeless kids. They didn't even have two pairs of socks that matched. Jeremy immediately took the boys to the barbershop to get haircuts because they looked so raggedy.

Since the boys were only supposed to be here for a couple of weeks, we had Tabatha sleep in the bed with Ashley, and we bought an air mattress for one of the boys. I took some time off to show the boys around Chicago and to spend time with them while they were here. I was frustrated with Laura again because she had never even spoken to me on the phone. She would only communicate with Jeremy. You would think she would want to talk to me since she was sending her kids to visit my kids and me, but no.

The girls enjoyed the boys' company, and Tabatha loved having her brothers around because they played outside and hung out with her. Ashley, as a typical teenage girl, did not want to play all the time. One day, Ashley called me at work, screaming on the phone. The boys had played a prank on her, taking her cell phone and hiding it. Ashley was screaming and crying. The boys called Jeremy on the phone and said they were having fun. Jeremy and I got on the phone and started yelling at each other. He said, "They are boys, just having fun." I was yelling because Ashley is not used to anyone touching her things, and they should leave her stuff alone. This was the first sign that I was looking forward to these two weeks being over soon.

In addition to the boys and all their roughhousing, I was not used to having all girls in the house. These boys were messy, and they did not believe in cleaning up after themselves. They also ate so much. We could not keep enough food in the house. They ate all the cereal, oatmeal, drank all the Kool-Aid and juice, and finished all the snacks. They loved to wrestle, and they even put a hole in my kitchen wall while playing around. I think we were both ready for them to go back home, but Laura had not called to say anything about a return date. It was about three weeks before school started, so it should be soon.

Finally, about two weeks before school started, Laura called Jeremy and said she needed the boys to stay with us indefinitely. She said she had already put all their school records, Social Security numbers, birth certificates, and everything we needed to get them registered for school in a FedEx box, which would arrive soon. She said she needed time to get herself together and that she wanted the boys to stay with us permanently.

Again, she did not speak with me about anything. I didn't know what the kids' favorite cereal was or whether they had any allergies. I didn't know their favorite color or anything else about them. We didn't have another bedroom, so now the girls had to give up their rooms, and we all had to make room for everyone to live comfortably. Also, it was two weeks before school started, so I now had to register them and buy back-to-school supplies for four kids instead of two. I was angry and felt that this was completely unfair to the girls and me. I was upset that this woman could just give her kids away and go about her life while I was stuck figuring out how to feed them. Jeremy was frustrated too, but he couldn't do or say much because they were his kids. We were just getting used to paying our new bills as homeowners, and now we had two more kids to take care of.

This was going to be a true test of our relationship because we had already been arguing more since the boys arrived. Now, the stress of blending this family and the extra strain on our finances was going to challenge us further. I believed Laura did this on purpose and that she was jealous of our marriage. However, what could I do? The boys were here, and we had to make room for them. I had to accept them, just like Jeremy accepted my girls.

Whew, I didn't know how this was going to work out.

.

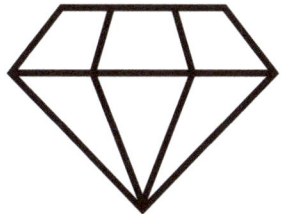

ABOUT THE AUTHOR

Anna Johnson is a devoted wife, mother, sister, aunt, and friend. She has been married to her husband for nearly twenty years, and together they share a blended family of five children and one beautiful granddaughter. Born and raised on the West Side of Chicago, Anna now resides with her family in the far western suburbs.

The youngest of five children, Anna grew up in a close-knit family. Though her oldest brother passed away in 1980, she remains connected to her two sisters and brother. Both of her parents are also deceased, but their legacy lives on—especially her father's, who owned one of the oldest Black-owned flower shops in Chicago.

Anna holds a bachelor's degree in Communications and a master's degree in Information Technology and Privacy Law from The John Marshall Law School. She has spent more than 30 years working in higher education and currently serves in Graduate Medical Education. She also has experience teaching Introduction to College Writing at the community college level, reflecting her ongoing passion for learning and helping others grow.

This is her first book, and she looks forward to writing many more that will inspire readers to grow, learn, strive, and strengthen their faith in God.

A diamond does not start out dazzling; it begins as plain coal. Through time, intense heat, and pressure, it becomes one of Earth's most prized treasures. Like diamonds, greatness is born from life's toughest moments. So, when things get rough, remember that pressure does not break you; it molds you. Stay resilient.

Keep shining!

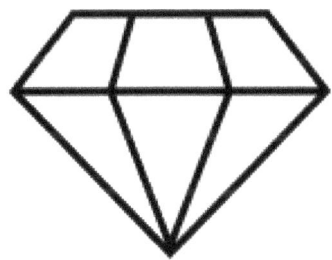

www.ingramcontent.com/pod-product-compliance
Lightning Source LLC
Chambersburg PA
CBHW051644120626
46551CB00015B/2206